Multi-Engine Oral Exam Guide

Third Edition

The comprehensive guide to prepare you for the FAA Oral Exam

by Michael D. Hayes

Aviation Supplies & Academics, Inc.
Newcastle, Washington

Multi-Engine Oral Exam Guide
Third Edition

Aviation Supplies & Academics, Inc.
7005 132nd Place SE
Newcastle, Washington 98059-3153

© 1994–2000 Aviation Supplies & Academics, Inc.
All rights reserved. Third Edition published 1998. Second Printing 2000.

ISBN 1-56027-403-4
ASA-OEG-ME3

Printed in the United States of America

03   02   01   00   9   8   7   6   5   4   3   2

Library of Congress Catloging-in-Publication Data:

Hayes, Michael D.
     Multi-engine oral exam guide : the comprehensive guide to prepare you
for the FAA oral exam / by Michael D. Hayes.
          p.   cm.
     "ASA-OEG-ME"—T.p. verso
     Includes index.
     ISBN 1-56027-193-0
     1. Multiengine flying—Examinations, questions, etc. 2. Air pilots—
Licenses—United States. I. Title.
     TL711.T85H39 1994
     629.132'5216'076—dc20   94-5808
                                                         CIP

This guide is dedicated to the many talented students, pilots, and flight instructors I have had the opportunity to work with over the years. Also, special thanks to Mark Hayes and many others who supplied the patience, encouragement, and understanding necessary to complete the project.

— M.D.H.

Contents

Continued

4   **Multi-Engine Maneuvers**

Introduction

The *Multi-Engine Oral Exam Guide* is a comprehensive guide designed for pilots training for the Multi-Engine Rating. This guide was originally designed for use in a Part 141 flight school, but it quickly became popular with those training under Part 61 who are not affiliated with an approved school. The guide also proves beneficial to pilots who wish to refresh their knowledge or who are preparing for a biennial flight review.

The *Multi-Engine Oral Exam Guide* is divided into four main sections. The first three sections represent the basic subject areas in which knowledge must be demonstrated by the applicant before issuance of the Multi-Engine Rating. The fourth section is a general review of the procedures and maneuvers required during the flight portion of the checkride. You should review the Practical Test Standards applicable to your particular certification check (i.e., Commercial, Instrument), in addition to the material in this section.

An FAA examiner may ask questions at any time during the practical test to determine the applicant has the required knowledge. The result of intensive post-multi checkride de-briefings, this book provides the most consistent questions asked, along with the information necessary for a knowledgeable response.

Continued

The guide may be supplemented with other comprehensive study materials as noted in parentheses after each question. For example: (FAA-H-8083-1). The abbreviations for these materials and their titles are listed below. Be sure to use the latest revision of these references when reviewing for the test.

14 CFR Part 23	*Airworthiness Standards: Normal, Utility, Acrobatic, and Commuter Category Airplanes*
14 CFR Part 43	*Maintenance, Preventive Maintenance, Rebuilding, and Alteration*
14 CFR Part 61	*Certification: Pilots, Flight Instructors, and Ground Instructors*
14 CFR Part 91	*General Operating and Flight Rules*
AC 61-23	*Pilot's Handbook of Aeronautical Knowledge*
AC 91-67	*Minimum Equipment requirements for General Aviation Operations under 14 CFR Part 91*
FAA-H-8083-1	*Aircraft Weight and Balance Handbook*
FAA-H-8083-3	*Airplane Flying Handbook*
FAA-P-8740-19	*Flying Light Twins Safely*
FAA-S-8081-14M	*Private Pilot Airplane Multi-Engine Land Practical Test Standards*
AIM	*Aeronautical Information Manual*
POH	*Pertinent Pilot Operating Handbooks*
AFM	*FAA-Approved Flight Manuals*

Most of the books listed above are reprinted by ASA and available from aviation retailers worldwide.

A review of the information presented within this guide should provide the necessary preparation for the FAA Multi-Engine Land practical test.

Were you asked a question during your checkride that was not covered in this book? If so, please send the question to ASA. We are constantly striving to improve our publications to meet the industry needs.

e-mail: asa@asa2fly.com   7005 132nd Place SE
Fax: 425.235.0128   Newcastle, WA 98059-3153

Multi-Engine Operations

1

A. Normal Procedures

1. What documents are required on board a multi-engine aircraft? (14 CFR 91.9, 91.203)

A irworthiness Certificate

R egistration Certificate

O wner's manual or operating limitations

W eight and balance data

2. What are the required tests and inspections to be performed on multi-engine aircraft? (Include inspections for IFR.) (14 CFR 91.171, 91.203, 91.207, 91.411, 91.413)

The same as for all aircraft. Obviously, multi-engine aircraft will have two engine logs instead of one.

a. The aircraft must have an annual inspection. If operated for hire or rental, it must also have a 100-hour inspection. A record must be kept in the aircraft/engine logbooks.

b. The pitot/static system must have been checked within the preceding 24 calendar months. A record must be kept in the aircraft logbook.

c. The transponder must have been checked within the preceding 24 calendar months. A record must be kept in the aircraft logbook.

d. The altimeter must have been checked within the preceding 24 calendar months. A record must be kept in the aircraft logbook.

e. The VOR must have been checked within the preceding 30 days. A record must be kept in a bound logbook.

f. If operations require an emergency locator transmitter (ELT), it must be inspected within 12 calendar months after the last inspection. The batteries must be replaced or recharged if ELT has been in use for 1 cumulative hour or 50 percent of their

Continued

useful life. Date for replacing or recharging the battery must be legibly marked on the outside of the transmitter and entered in the aircraft maintenance record.

Note: Be able to locate the last 100-hour/annual inspections in the aircraft and engine logbooks, and determine when the next inspections are due. Also be able to locate all required inspections for instruments and equipment necessary for legal VFR/IFR flight.

3. Is taxiing a multi-engine airplane significantly different than taxiing a single-engine airplane? (FAA-H-8083-3)

No, it is generally the same. The following general guidelines may be used:

a. Brakes and throttles are used to control momentum.

b. Steering is done primarily with the steerable nose wheel.

c. Directional control may also be obtained through use of differential power, if necessary.

d. Plan ahead. Multi-engine airplanes are heavier, larger, and more powerful. They require more time and distance to stop.

e. Also, due to size, pilot perspective may change, requiring additional vigilance to avoid obstacles, other aircraft, or bystanders.

4. How can a pilot use differential power during taxiing?

While taxiing, a tight turn to the right, for example, may be accomplished by reducing power on the right engine and increasing power on the left engine while applying right rudder/brake. Also, in a crosswind condition, differential power assists in controlling direction. Power should be applied on the upwind engine causing a turning moment away from the crosswind.

5. What procedure is recommended concerning use of checklists in multi-engine airplanes? (FAA-H-8083-3)

In airplanes which require a copilot, or in which a second pilot is available, it is a good practice for the second pilot to read the checklist and the pilot-in-command to check each item by actually touching the control or device and repeating the instrument reading or prescribed control position in question under the careful observation of the pilot calling out the checklist items. Even when no copilot is present, the pilot should form the habit of touching, pointing to, or operating each item as it is read from the checklist.

6. What are the three most critical phases of flight in a multi-engine airplane?

Takeoff, initial climb, and landing. During takeoff and climb the aircraft is usually in its most vulnerable state—low altitude, slow airspeed, and heaviest operating weight. During landing, the aircraft is also operating at a relatively slow airspeed and low altitude, leaving little room for error.

7. What are the first and second priorities for a multi-engine pilot during the takeoff roll? (FAA-H-8083-3)

The multi-engine pilot's primary concern on all takeoffs is reaching the engine-out minimum control speed before liftoff. Until this speed is achieved, directional control of the airplane in flight will be impossible after the failure of one engine, unless power is reduced immediately on the operating engine.

The multi-engine pilot's second concern on takeoff is the attainment of the single-engine best rate-of-climb speed (V_{YSE}) in the least amount of time. This is the airspeed which will provide the greatest rate of climb when operating with one engine out and feathered (if possible), or the slowest rate of descent.

8. What is the recommended flap position for a normal takeoff? Short-field takeoff? (Aircraft Flight Manual)

No flaps for a normal takeoff. Fifteen degrees for a short-field (maximum performance) takeoff.

9. Discuss a normal takeoff and climb procedure in a multi-engine airplane. (FAA-H-8083-3)

An efficient climb procedure is one in which the airplane leaves the ground slightly above V_{MC}, accelerates quickly to V_Y (best rate of climb) and climbs at V_Y. The climb at V_Y should be made with both engines set to maximum takeoff power until reaching a safe single-engine maneuvering altitude (minimum of approximately 500 feet above field elevation or as dictated by airplane performance capability and/or local obstacles). At this point, power may be reduced to the allowable maximum continuous power setting (METO—maximum except takeoff) or less, and any desired enroute climb speed may then be established.

10. When is the gear retracted in a normal takeoff?

Normally, the landing gear should not be retracted until the following conditions have been met:

a. No more usable runway is available in the event of an aborted takeoff.

b. A positive rate climb is established.

11. At what point should a pre-landing checklist be completed in a standard traffic pattern? (FAA-H-8083-3)

The pre-landing checklist should be completed by the time the airplane is on base leg so that the pilot may direct full attention to the approach and landing.

12. Where in the traffic pattern should the propellers be set to a low pitch/high rpm condition? Why?

On final, the propeller controls should be set to low pitch/high rpm. This action should be accomplished so that, in the event a go-around is necessary, the propellers are already set for maximum power application.

13. Can an aircraft operator allow flight operations to be conducted in an aircraft with known inoperative equipment? (AC 91-67, 14 CFR 91.213)

Part 91 describes acceptable methods for the operation of an aircraft with certain inoperative instruments and equipment which are not essential for safe flight. These acceptable methods of operation are:

a. With a Minimum Equipment List (MEL), as authorized by 14 CFR 91.213(a).

b. Without an MEL under 14 CFR 91.213(d).

14. What are Minimum Equipment Lists? (AC 91-67)

The Minimum Equipment List (MEL) is a precise listing of instruments, equipment, and procedures that allows an aircraft to be operated under specific conditions with inoperative equipment. The MEL is the specific inoperative-equipment document for a particular make and model aircraft by serial and registration numbers; e.g., BE-200, N12345. The FAA-approved MEL includes only those items of equipment the administrator designates that may be inoperative yet maintain an acceptable level of safety by appropriate conditions and limitations.

15. If an aircraft is not being operated under a MEL, how can you determine which instruments and equipment on board can be inoperative and the aircraft still be legal for flight? (14 CFR 91.213)

The inoperative instruments must not be:

a. Part of the VFR-day type certification instruments and equipment prescribed in the applicable airworthiness regulations under which the aircraft was type certificated.

b. Indicated as required on the aircraft's equipment list, or on the Kinds of Operations Equipment List, for the kind of flight operation being conducted.

16. What is an aircraft equipment list, and where is it found?
(AC 91-67)

The aircraft equipment list is an inventory of equipment installed
by the manufacturer or operator on a particular aircraft. It is
usually found with the weight and balance data.

**17. What length of time can an aircraft be flown with
inoperative equipment on board?** (AC 91-67)

An operator may defer maintenance on inoperative equipment that
has been deactivated or removed and placarded inoperative. When
the aircraft is due for inspection in accordance with the regulations,
the operator should have all inoperative items repaired or replaced.
If an owner does not want specific inoperative equipment repaired,
then the maintenance person must check each item to see if it
conforms to the requirements of 14 CFR 91.213. The maintenance
person must ensure that each item of inoperative equipment that is
to remain inoperative is placarded appropriately.

B. Aerodynamics

**1. Discuss the use of power during approach and landing
in a multi-engine airplane.** (FAA-H-8083-3)

Multi-engine airplanes characteristically have steeper gliding
angles because of their relatively high wing loading and greater
drag of wing flaps and landing gear when extended. For this
reason, power is normally used throughout the approach to shallow
the approach angle and prevent a high rate of sink.

**2. Discuss the effects of P-factor in a multi-engine
airplane.** (FAA-H-8083-3)

In most U.S.-designed light-twins, both engines rotate to the right
(clockwise) when viewed from the rear, and both engines develop
an equal amount of thrust. At low airspeed and high power
conditions, the downward moving propeller blade of each engine
develops more thrust than the upward moving blade. This asymmetric propeller thrust, or "P-factor," results in a center of thrust at

the right side of each engine. The turning (or yawing) force of the
right engine is greater than the left engine because the center of
thrust is much farther away from the center line of the fuselage—
it has a longer level arm. Thus, when the right engine is operative
and the left engine is inoperative, the turning or yawing force is
greater than the opposite situation of an operative left engine and
an inoperative right engine. In other words, directional control may
be difficult when the left engine (the critical engine) is suddenly
made inoperative.

**3. What are the operational advantages of an aircraft
equipped with counter-rotating propellers?**
(FAA-H-8083-3)

The main advantage of an aircraft equipped with counter-rotating
propellers is the distinct advantage of not having a critical engine.
The thrust line of either engine is the same distance from the
centerline of the fuselage, so there will be no difference in yaw
effect between loss of the left or the right engine.

C. Determining Performance and Limitations

**1. Define the following speeds and their value for your
aircraft.** (14 CFR Part 1)

V_{FE} — Maximum flaps extended speed

V_{LE} — Maximum landing gear extended speed

V_{LO} — Maximum landing gear operating speed

V_{NE} — Never-exceed speed

V_{MC} — Minimum control speed with critical engine inoperative

V_{NO} — Maximum structural cruising speed

V_{SO} — Stalling speed or the minimum steady flight speed in the
landing configuration

V_S — Stalling speed or the minimum steady flight speed at
which the aircraft is controllable

V_{S1} — Stalling speed or the minimum steady flight speed
obtained in a specific configuration

Continued

V_X — Speed for best angle of climb

V_{XSE} — Speed for best angle of climb single-engine

V_Y — Speed for best rate of climb

V_{YSE} — Speed for best rate of climb single-engine

V_{SSE} — Safe single-engine speed

V_A — Design maneuvering speed

2. When is use of the safe single-engine speed (V_{SSE}) recommended? (FAA-P-8740-19)

V_{SSE} is specified by the airplane manufacturer in the new hand-books and is the minimum speed at which to perform intentional engine cuts. Use of V_{SSE} is intended to reduce the accident poten-tial from loss of control after engine cuts at or near minimum control speed. V_{MC} demonstrations are necessary in training but should only be made at a safe altitude above the terrain and with the power reduction on one engine made at or above V_{SSE}.

3. Define "accelerate-stop distance." (FAA-H-8083-3)

The accelerate-stop distance is the total distance required to accelerate the multi-engine airplane to a specified speed, and assuming failure of an engine at the instant that speed is attained, to bring the airplane to a full stop on the remaining runway.

4. Is a takeoff advisable if the accelerate-stop distance exceeds the available runway distance? Why?

No, it's not advisable. In the event of an engine failure during the takeoff ground run, chances would be minimal that the aircraft could be brought to a full stop on the remaining runway.

5. Do the regulations prohibit a pilot from attempting a takeoff in a multi-engine airplane if the accelerate-stop distance is greater than the total runway length? (14 CFR Parts 91, 121, 135)

No, if operations are conducted under 14 CFR Part 91. Operations conducted under 14 CFR Parts 121 and 135 prohibit this type of operation.

6. What procedures are followed if the accelerate-stop distance exceeds the runway length and/or the density altitude is higher than the single-engine service ceiling?

A takeoff under these conditions would be inadvisable. If, for some reason, a takeoff must be made, an alternate plan of action should be thought-out well in advance, and should include:

a. A review of emergency landing areas or other runways near the departure runway;

b. A review of engine-out performance speeds and procedures;

c. Due consideration to a reduction in baggage, fuel, and/or passengers to increase single-engine performance.

7. Define "accelerate-go distance." (FAA-H-8083-3)

The accelerate-go distance is the distance required to accelerate to liftoff speed and, assuming failure of an engine at the moment initial liftoff speed is attained, to continue the takeoff on the remaining engine to a height of 50 feet.

8. Why is the information provided by accelerate-go charts important to safe multi-engine operations? (FAA-P-8740-19)

Review the information provided by accelerate-go charts carefully. No airplane is capable of climbing out on one engine under all weight, pressure altitude and temperature conditions. Know before you take the actual runway whether you can maintain control and climb out if you lose an engine while the gear is still down.

9. What performance factors should be considered when planning a takeoff in a multi-engine airplane?

Competent pilots will plan the takeoff in sufficient detail to be able to take immediate action if an engine fails during the takeoff process. The pilot will be thoroughly familiar with the:

a. Normal takeoff ground run distance

b. Ground run distance required to clear a 50-foot obstacle

c. Surrounding terrain and obstructions

d. Nearby emergency landing areas in the event of engine failure

e. Accelerate-stop distance

f. Accelerate-go distance

g. Existing density altitude and single-engine service ceiling

h. Alternate plan of action

10. If two pilots are present, what information should be reviewed immediately prior to takeoff in a multi-engine airplane? (FAA-H-8083-3)

If the crew consists of two pilots, it is recommended that the pilot-in-command brief the other pilot on takeoff procedures prior to takeoff. This briefing should consist of at least the following:

a. Minimum control speed (V_{MC})

b. Rotation speed (V_R)

c. Liftoff speed (V_{LOF})

d. Single engine best rate-of-climb speed (V_{YSE})

e. All engine best rate-of-climb speed (V_Y)

f. Procedures to follow if an engine failure occurs prior to and after V_{MC}.

11. Discuss the procedures to be used for a short-field takeoff in a light twin that has a best angle-of-climb speed (two engine) below V_{MC}. (FAA-H-8083-3)

In some light twins V_X is below V_{MC}. In this case, if the climb were made at V_X and a sudden power failure occurred on one engine, the pilot would not be able to control the airplane unless

power were reduced on the operating eng.
impossible situation because it would not b
could clear the obstacle with one engine ope.
some reduced power setting. If the published b
speed (V_X) is less than V_{MC} plus 5, then it is rec
less than V_{MC} plus 5 knots be used. During the tak
airspeed reaches the best angle of climb or V_{MC} plu.   .iever
is higher, the airplane should be rotated to establish a. .ngle of
attack that will cause the airplane to lift off and climb at that speed.

12. What four main factors determine climb performance? (FAA-P-8740-19)

Airspeed—too little or too much will decrease climb performance.

Drag—created by gear, flaps, cowl flaps, propeller and airspeed.

Power—the amount available in excess of that needed for level flight.

Weight—passengers, baggage and fuel load greatly affect climb performance.

13. Overall climb performance is reduced by what value in an engine-out emergency? Why? (FAA-P-8740-19)

Climb performance depends on an excess of power over that required for level flight. Loss of power from one engine obviously represents a 50 percent loss of power but, in virtually all light twins, climb performance is reduced by at least 80 percent. The amount of power required for level flight depends on how much drag must be overcome to sustain level flight. It's obvious that if drag is increased because the gear and flaps are down and the propeller is windmilling, more power will be required. Not so obvious, however, is the fact that drag increases as the square of the airspeed while the power required to maintain that speed increases as the cube of the airspeed.

operational advantages are achieved through use of a cruise-climb airspeed versus a best rate-of-climb airspeed during an extended climb?

a. A higher ground speed (forward speed) will be achieved, reducing the total time en route (usually an important factor in cross-country trips).

b. Only a small reduction in rate of climb will occur.

c. An increase in forward visibility is achieved during climb-out.

d. Engine cooling is increased due to a higher forward speed.

15. Why are some multi-engine aircraft required to have performance capabilities that require a positive single-engine climb rate? (14 CFR Part 23)

In the interest of safety, the FAA requires that all turboprop, turbojet, large aircraft (10 or more passengers), or aircraft involved in air taxi operations be required to demonstrate continued takeoff capability with one engine inoperative.

16. In addition to turboprop, turbojet and large aircraft, what other type of multi-engine aircraft are required to have positive single-engine climb rates? (14 CFR Part 23)

Part 23 sets the standards for certification of light aircraft (12,500 pounds or less). Multi-engine aircraft are further subdivided into two categories:

Aircraft requiring single-engine climb performance:

(These aircraft must demonstrate single-engine climb capability at 5,000 feet (ISA) with one engine inoperative and feathered and the aircraft in a clean configuration.) Rate of climb required = 0.027 times V_{S0} squared.

a. Aircraft weighing 6,000 pounds or less with a V_{S0} stall speed greater than 61 knots CAS

b. Aircraft weighing more than 6,000 pounds with a V_{S0} stall speed greater than 61 knots

Aircraft NOT requiring single-engine climb performance:

No requirements for climb rate except that single-engine performance at 5,000 feet (ISA) be determined.

a. Aircraft weighing 6,000 pounds or less with a V_{S0} stall speed 61 knots or less.

17. Define the term "service ceiling." (FAA-H-8083-3)

The service ceiling is the maximum density altitude at which use of best rate-of-climb airspeed will result in a climb rate of 100 fpm.

18. What factors affect the effective service ceiling of a multi-engine airplane? (FAA-H-8083-3)

The service ceiling will be affected by:

a. Weight

b. Pressure altitude

c. Temperature

19. Define the term "absolute service ceiling." (FAA-H-8083-3)

The absolute service ceiling is defined as the maximum density altitude the airplane is capable of attaining or maintaining. It is also the density altitude where V_X and V_Y are equal.

20. Define "single-engine service ceiling." (FAA-H-8083-3)

The single-engine service ceiling is defined as the maximum altitude at which the rate of climb produced is 50 fpm with one engine inoperative.

21. What happens to V_{YSE} and V_{XSE} as aircraft altitude increases?

V_{XSE} increases and V_{YSE} decreases.

22. Define "single-engine absolute ceiling."

The single-engine absolute ceiling is defined as the maximum density altitude the airplane is capable of attaining and maintaining with the critical engine inoperative and the propeller feathered. It is also the altitude at which V_{XSE} and V_{YSE} are equal.

23. Is a takeoff advisable if the density altitude at an airport is higher than the single-engine service ceiling?

No. Available alternatives are few since the aircraft would be unable to climb or even maintain altitude in the event of an engine failure on takeoff. Know before you take the runway whether you can maintain control and climb out if you lose an engine while the gear is still down.

24. Do the regulations prohibit a pilot from attempting a takeoff in a multi-engine airplane if the airport density altitude is higher than the single-engine service ceiling? (14 CFR Part 91)

No, if operations are being conducted under 14 CFR Part 91.

25. If an engine failure should occur on takeoff at a field where the density altitude is higher than the single-engine service ceiling, what performance can be expected with one engine out?

For most light twins, none.

26. During flight planning, what important consideration should be made concerning the single-engine service ceiling as related to the enroute portion of a flight? (FAA-P-8740-19)

The single-engine service ceiling chart should always be used during flight planning to determine whether the airplane, as loaded, can maintain the Minimum Enroute Altitude (MEA) if IFR, or terrain clearance if VFR, following an engine failure.

27. Be capable of determining the following for your aircraft:
(Aircraft Flight Manual)

a. Total takeoff distance required to clear a 50-foot obstacle.

b. Accelerate-stop distance if an engine failure occurs at takeoff decision speed.

c. Accelerate-go distance if an engine failure occurs at takeoff decision speed.

d. Total time, distance traveled, and fuel burned in a standard cruise climb to 10,000 feet.

e. Fuel consumption, range, and endurance of the training aircraft.

f. Time and point of descent from cruise altitude to pattern altitude for the training aircraft.

D. Weight and Balance

1. What performance characteristics will be adversely affected when an aircraft has been overloaded?
(AC 61-23C)

a. Higher takeoff speed

b. Longer takeoff run

c. Reduced rate and angle of climb

d. Lower maximum altitude

e. Shorter range

f. Reduced cruising speed

g. Reduced maneuverability

h. Higher stalling speed

i. Higher landing speed

j. Longer landing roll

2. What effect does a forward center of gravity have on an aircraft's flight characteristics? (AC 61-23C)

Higher stall speed—stalling angle of attack reached at a higher speed due to increased wing loading.

Slower cruise speed—increased drag; greater angle of attack required to maintain altitude.

More stable—when angle of attack increased, airplane tends to reduce angle of attack; longitudinal stability.

Lower V_{MC}—rudder more effective.

Greater back elevator pressure required—longer takeoff roll; higher approach speeds and problems with landing flare.

3. What effect does an aft center of gravity have on an aircraft's flight characteristics? (AC 61-23C)

Lower stall speed—less wing loading.

Higher cruise speed—reduced drag; smaller angle of attack required to maintain altitude.

Less stable—stall and spin recovery more difficult; when angle of attack is increased it tends to result in additional increased angle of attack.

Higher V_{MC}—rudder less effective.

4. Define the following terms and their value for your aircraft. (FAA-H-8083-1)

Maximum takeoff weight—the maximum allowable weight at the start of the takeoff run. Some aircraft are approved for loading to a greater weight (ramp or taxi) only to allow for fuel to burn off during ground operations. The takeoff weight for a particular flight may be limited to a lesser weight when runway length, atmospheric conditions, or other variables are adverse.

Maximum landing weight—the maximum weight at which the aircraft may normally be landed. The maximum landing weight may be limited to a lesser weight when runway length or atmospheric conditions are adverse.

Basic empty weight—weight of the airframe, engines, and all items of operating equipment that have fixed locations and are permanently installed in the aircraft. It includes optional and special equipment, fixed ballast, hydraulic fluid, and undrainable (residual) fuel and oil. When oil is used for propeller feathering, such oil is included as residual oil.

Maximum allowable zero fuel weight—the maximum weight authorized for the aircraft not including fuel load. Zero fuel weight for each particular flight is the operating weight plus the payload.

5. Explain the importance of "maximum takeoff weight." (FAA-H-8083-1)

As compared to the "gross weight" of the aircraft, the "maximum takeoff weight" will usually be the more restrictive of the two. It will provide the pilot with the option to accelerate/stop or accelerate/go after an engine failure on the available runway, as well as guarantee an initial climb gradient that will clear all obstacles (considering atmosphere).

6. Define the term "payload." (FAA-H-8083-1)

"Payload" refers to the "Useful" load of the aircraft which consists of the pilot, passengers, baggage, usable fuel and drainable oil.

7. Be capable of calculating a weight and balance computation for your aircraft using the following data: (Aircraft Flight Manual)

Pilot and Copilot (be sure to obtain the examiner's weight)
Passengers
Fuel and Oil
Baggage

Also, calculate a weight and balance computation after 2 hours of flight.

Flight Principles: Engine Inoperative

2

A. Factors Affecting Single-Engine Flight

1. What factors affect V_{MC}?

a. CG position

b. Weight

c. Density altitude

d. Landing gear position

e. Position of flaps

f. Propeller (windmilling or feathered)

g. Sideslip condition

2. What factors would cause V_{MC} to be higher?

a. Rearward CG location

b. Decrease in weight

c. Decrease in density altitude (increase in air density)

d. Landing gear position: depending on the manufacturer, the retracted position could cause the V_{MC} to change.

e. Flaps position: depending on the manufacturer, the retracted position could affect V_{MC}.

f. Propeller windmilling

g. Sideslip condition (lack of bank towards operative engine)

3. Explain why the movement of the center of gravity (CG) affects V_{MC}. (FAA-H-8083-3)

V_{MC} is greater when the CG is at the rearmost allowable position. Since the airplane rotates around the center of gravity, the moments are measured using that point as a reference. A rearward CG would not affect a thrust moment, but would shorten the arm to the center of the rudder's horizontal lift which would mean a higher force (airspeed) would be required to counteract the engine-out yaw. Generally, the CG range of most light twins is short enough that the effect on V_{MC} is relatively small, but it is a factor that should be considered.

4. Why does a change in weight affect V_{MC}?

V_{MC} is unaffected by weight in straight and level flight. V_{MC} will be affected by the aircraft's weight in turning (banked) flight. When an aircraft is banked, a component of the aircraft weight acts along with the horizontal component of lift to create a more effective sideslip toward the operative engine. For a given bank angle, the greater the aircraft's weight, the lower the aircraft's V_{MC}.

5. Why does a change in density altitude affect V_{MC}? (FAA-H-8083-3)

For an airplane with non-supercharged engines, V_{MC} decreases as density altitude increases. Consequently, directional control can be maintained at a lower airspeed than at sea level. This is because since power decreases with altitude, the thrust moment of the operating engine lessens, thereby reducing the need for the yawing force of the rudder.

6. Explain why a change in landing gear position could affect V_{MC}.

Part 23 certification requires gear to be up when determining V_{MC}. The change in CG caused by the forward extension of the nose gear increases the arm length from the CG to the rudder and makes rudder deflection more effective, resulting in a tendency to *reduce* V_{MC}. However, the prop slipstream hitting the gear down has a tendency to increase drag and therefore *increase* V_{MC}. Depending on the airplane manufacturer, the landing gear position may result in a change to V_{MC}, although this change will most likely be negligible.

7. Explain why extending the flaps could affect V_{MC}.

It is generally accepted that V_{MC} will be slightly lower with flaps extended. Extended flaps will increase both drag and lift. The drag produced by the extended flap on the operative engine side will tend to oppose the yawing motion of that engine. The overall effect is a decrease in yaw and less required rudder force to counteract that yaw. Since less rudder force is required to counteract the yawing moment, less airspeed is required to produce that rudder force. V_{MC} may be slightly lower, depending on the manufacturer.

8. How does a windmilling propeller affect V_{MC}? (FAA-H-8083-3)

A windmilling propeller will generate significant drag, resulting in less directional control and a higher V_{MC}.

9. How does a sideslip condition affect V_{MC}? (FAA-H-8083-3)

During engine-out flight the large rudder deflection required to counteract the asymmetric thrust also results in a "lateral lift" force on the vertical fin. The lateral "lift" represents an unbalanced side force on the airplane which is counteracted by allowing the airplane to accelerate sideways until the lateral drag caused by the sideslip equals the rudder "lift" force. The wings will be level, the ball in the turn and slip indicator will be centered and the airplane will be in a moderate sideslip toward the inoperative engine. A sideslip condition will result in the following:

a. The relative wind blowing on the inoperative engine side of the vertical fin tends to increase the asymmetric moment caused by the failure of one engine;

b. The resulting sideslip severely degrades stall characteristics;

c. The greater the rudder deflection required to balance the extra moment and the sideslip drag cause a significant reduction in climb and/or acceleration capability;

d. V_{MC} will be higher.

10. During a training flight, what conditions would make a V_{MC} demonstration inadvisable? (FAA-H-8083-3)

Since V_{MC} is a function of power (which decreases with altitude), it is possible for the airplane to reach a stall speed prior to loss of directional control. It must be understood that there is a certain density altitude above which the stalling speed is higher than the engine-out minimum control speed. During a typical V_{MC} demonstration, with one engine feathered and the aircraft slowing to V_{MC}, a stall would occur first, followed by a very strong tendency for the aircraft to roll. This situation would almost certainly guarantee a spin condition which could be difficult to correct. When this

Continued

density altitude (due to high elevations or temperatures) exists close to the ground or at altitude, an effective flight demonstration of loss of directional control may be hazardous and should not be attempted.

11. Define the term "critical engine." (14 CFR Part 1)

The "critical engine" is the engine whose failure would most adversely affect the performance or handling qualities of the airplane.

12. Do all multi-engine aircraft have a critical engine? (FAA-H-8083-3)

Most U.S. light twins are configured with a critical engine. Some aircraft, however, have counter-rotating propellers which eliminate the critical engine factor. These aircraft are equipped with engines turning in opposite directions; that is, the left engine and propeller turn clockwise and the right engine and propeller turn counterclockwise. With this arrangement, the thrust line of either engine is the same distance from the centerline of the fuselage, so there will be no difference in yaw effect between loss of the left or right engine.

13. On most multi-engine aircraft, what engine is normally considered the critical engine? (FAA-H-8083-3)

The critical engine on most U.S. light twins is the left engine, as its failure requires the most rudder force to overcome yaw.

14. Arrange the following in order of least amount of drag to most amount of drag contributed in an engine-out situation:
- **Flaps**
- **Landing gear**
- **Windmilling propeller**
- **Flight control position**

a. Flight control positions (to counteract yawing and rolling tendencies)—approximate loss 100 fpm.

b. Windmilling propeller—approximate loss 200 to 300 fpm.

c. Landing gear extended—approximate loss 300 to 400 fpm.

d. Flaps extended fully—approximate loss 300 to 400 fpm.

Note: The above performance values will vary for different aircraft. For accuracy, you should review your particular Aircraft Flight Manual.

15. What speed does the blue line on an airspeed indicator designate? (FAA-H-8083-3)

Best Single-Engine Rate-of-Climb Speed (V_{YSE}), which delivers the greatest gain in altitude in the shortest possible time with one engine inoperative.

16. What speed does the red line on an airspeed indicator designate? (FAA-H-8083-3)

Minimum Control Speed Critical Engine Inoperative (V_{MC}) indicates the minimum control speed, airborne at sea level with the critical engine inoperative.

17. How is V_{MC} determined by the manufacturer? (14 CFR 23.149)

V_{MC} is the calibrated airspeed at which it is possible to maintain control of the airplane when the critical engine is suddenly made inoperative, and thereafter maintain straight flight at the same speed with an angle of bank of not more than 5 degrees. The method used to simulate critical engine failure must represent the most critical mode of powerplant failure expected in service with respect to controllability. V_{MC} for takeoff must not exceed 1.2 V_{S1}, where V_{S1} is determined at the maximum takeoff weight. V_{MC} must be determined with the most unfavorable weight and center of gravity position, and with the airplane airborne and ground effect negligible, for the takeoff configuration(s) with:

a. Maximum available takeoff power initially on each engine;

b. The airplane trimmed for takeoff;

c. Flaps in the takeoff position(s);

d. Landing gear retracted; and

e. All propeller controls in the recommended takeoff position throughout.

B. Directional Control

1. What three performance/control problems must a pilot deal with immediately after the loss of one engine on a multi-engine aircraft? (FAA-P-8740-19)

The loss of power on one engine affects both climb performance and controllability of any light twin. The following problems will occur:

a. Loss of climb performance (at least 80 percent);

b. A yawing moment towards the inoperative engine (due to asymmetric thrust);

c. A rolling moment towards the inoperative engine (due to loss of induced airflow).

2. Why does a multi-engine airplane become directionally uncontrollable during flight at an airspeed less than V_{MC}? (FAA-H-8083-3)

When one engine fails, the pilot must overcome the asymmetrical thrust (except on airplanes with centerline thrust) created by the operating engine by setting up a counteracting moment with the rudder. When the rudder is fully deflected, its yawing power will depend upon the velocity of airflow across the rudder, which in turn is dependent upon the airspeed. As the airplane decelerates, it will reach a speed below which the rudder moment will no longer balance the thrust moment and directional control will be lost.

3. Why is flight below V_{MC} so dangerous? (FAA-H-8083-3)

With full power applied to the operating engine, as the airspeed drops below V_{MC}, the airplane tends to roll as well as yaw into the inoperative engine. This tendency becomes greater as the airspeed is further reduced, and since this tendency must be counteracted by aileron control, the yaw condition is aggravated further by aileron yaw (adverse yaw). If a stall should occur in this condition (highly likely), a violent roll into the dead engine may take place. Such an event near the ground could be disastrous.

4. Why does a multi-engine airplane with one engine inoperative roll in the direction of the inoperative engine? (FAA-P-8740-19)

Loss of power on one engine reduces the induced airflow from the propeller slipstream over that wing. As a result, total lift for that wing is substantially reduced, causing the airplane to roll in the direction of the inoperative engine. Yaw also affects the lift distribution over the wing causing a roll toward the dead engine. These roll forces may be balanced by banking into the operative engine as well as application of rudder opposite to the direction of yaw.

5. What procedure is recommended for recovering from an inadvertent spin?

Most light twin-engine aircraft do not have favorable spin characteristics. As a result, recovery from an inadvertent spin may be difficult at best. The following procedure may be followed:

a. Reduce power on both engines.

b. Apply full rudder opposite the direction of rotation.

c. Apply positive forward elevator movement to break the stall.

d. If necessary, apply power to the engine on the inside of the direction of rotation.

e. Neutralize rudder pressure as rotation stops and recover from the dive with slow, steady, control movement.

If the above procedure fails to produce results, a combination of the above and full power to both engines may be beneficial in breaking the stalled condition. This should only be used as a last resort.

6. What are the reasons for feathering the propeller of an inoperative engine as soon as possible? (FAA-H-8083-3)

When an engine fails in flight, the movement of the airplane through the air tends to keep the propeller rotating, much like a windmill. Since the failed engine is no longer delivering power to the propeller to produce thrust, but instead may be absorbing

Continued

energy to overcome friction and compression of the engine, the drag of the windmilling propeller is significant and causes the airplane to yaw toward the failed engine. Also, in the event of an engine failure due to internal component failure, feathering the propeller may prevent further engine damage caused by a wind-milling propeller.

7. Why is it necessary to bank toward the operative engine in an engine-out emergency? (FAA-H-8083-3)

If the wings are kept level and the ball in the turn coordinator centered, the airplane will be in a moderate sideslip toward the inoperative engine, resulting in a substantial increase in V_{MC} and a significant reduction in climb and/or acceleration capability. By establishing a bank toward the operative engine, a component of the aircraft's weight is utilized to counteract the rudder-induced sideforce present in the sideslip. At a specific angle of bank, the airplane will be in a zero-sideslip condition, leading to adequate directional control as well as a substantial increase in engine-out performance (rate of climb). Decreasing the bank angle away from the operative engine increases V_{MC} at the rate of approximately 3 knots per degree of bank.

Note: Banking into the operative engine, beyond that necessary for a zero-sideslip condition, may increase rudder authority and assist in directional control initially but it will also *drastically* reduce the airplane's climb performance. Once directional control has been achieved, a reduction in bank angle, as necessary to achieve a zero-sideslip condition, must be established in order to obtain the necessary climb performance.

8. What is the correct amount of bank angle necessary in an engine-out emergency?

FAA research indicates that no one value for an optimum perfor-mance bank angle can be assigned to all aircraft. The particular aircraft's characteristics, weight, the density altitude, etc. are all factors which will influence the amount of bank necessary to establish a zero-sideslip condition in an engine-out emergency.

Experiments indicate that initially a bank angle of at least 5 degrees should be used to achieve the published V_{MC} value, and once the aircraft is under control, a reduction in bank angle to that value which will produce a zero-sideslip condition should be established for best performance. In absence of a known value for establishing a zero-sideslip condition for a particular airplane, a bank angle of 2 degrees or one-half ball-width deflection from the center of the turn coordinator may be used.

9. How much of an increase in V_{MC} will occur if a bank toward the operative engine is not established? (FAA-H-8083-3)

Flight tests have shown that holding the ball of the turn coordinator in the center while maintaining heading with the wings level drastically increases V_{MC} as much as 20 knots in some airplanes.

C. Engine-Out Operations

1. State three major causes of fatalities in engine-out emergencies.

Fatalities usually occur due to any one or combination of the following:

a. Loss of directional control

b. Loss of climb performance

c. Loss of flying airspeed

2. At what point, in terms of airspeed, is an engine failure on takeoff considered to be the most critical? (FAA-H-8083-3)

The most critical time for an engine-out condition in a multi-engine airplane is during the two- or three-second period immediately following the takeoff roll, while the airplane is accelerating to a safe engine failure speed.

3. Are most light multi-engine aircraft required to demonstrate a single-engine climb? (FAA-H-8083-3)

No; many pilots erroneously believe that because a light twin has two engines, it will continue to perform at least half as well with only one of those engines operating. There is nothing in 14 CFR Part 23, governing the certification of light twins, that requires an airplane to maintain altitude while in the takeoff configuration and with one engine inoperative. In fact, many current light twins are not required to do this with one engine inoperative in any configuration, even at sea level. This is of major significance in the operations of light twins certificated under Part 23. With regard to performance (but not controllability) in the takeoff or landing configuration, the light twin engine airplane is, in concept, merely a single-engine airplane with its power divided into two units.

4. What items on the single-engine emergency checklist should be committed to memory? (FAA-P-8740-19)

a. Maintain aircraft control and airspeed at all times. This is cardinal rule number one.

b. Usually apply maximum power to the operating engine. However, if the engine failure occurs during cruise or in a steep turn, you may elect to use only enough power to maintain a safe speed and altitude.

c. Reduce drag to an absolute minimum (retract flaps and landing gear).

5. If the airspeed is allowed to fall below V_{MC} during single-engine operation, what procedure should be followed? (FAA-H-8083-3)

If the airspeed should fall below V_{MC}, for whatever reason, power must be reduced on the operative engine and the airplane must be banked, as necessary, toward the operative engine if the airplane is to be safely controlled.

6. What immediate actions must be taken if loss of one engine occurs below V_{MC}? (FAA-H-8083-3)

If one engine fails prior to reaching V_{MC}, there is no choice but to close both throttles and bring the airplane to a stop. If the engine failure occurs after becoming airborne, the pilot must make an immediate decision to either continue flight or land.

7. What is the pilot's first priority following an engine failure? (FAA-H-8083-3)

Maintain aircraft control and airspeed.

8. Before feathering a suspected inoperative engine, what action should be taken first? (FAA-H-8083-3)

Verify which engine has failed by closing the throttle on the suspected dead engine.

9. In the event of an engine failure, what methods may be used to positively identify the inoperative engine? (FAA-H-8083-3)

An inoperative engine can be identified by:

a. A definite yaw and roll towards the inoperative engine.

b. The old adage "Dead Foot, Dead Engine" may be used. The foot that is not applying rudder pressure indicates the side on which the engine has failed.

c. Verification; retard the throttle of the suspected engine before shutting it down. If no change in control input is necessary, this is the side on which an engine has failed.

10. Which direction would the rudder be applied, if the right engine failed? (FAA-H-8083-3)

The aircraft would yaw to the right, requiring application of left rudder pressure immediately.

11. In the event of an engine failure in Instrument Meteorological Conditions, what methods should be used to positively identify the inoperative engine?

Methods used for inoperative engine identification in VMC also apply to flight in IMC. Give priority to scanning your flight instruments, ensuring that heading and airspeed are maintained. Control the heading primarily with rudder pressure. The airplane will yaw in the direction of the failed engine. The turn coordinator ball will swing towards the operative engine due to centrifugal force. As always, rudder pressure will assist you in identifying the inoperative engine (Dead Foot, Dead Engine).

12. When would V_{XSE} be used? (FAA-H-8083-3)

Best single-engine angle-of-climb speed will provide the maximum altitude gain in the shortest distance (steepest angle-of-climb). Use this speed when obstacles must be cleared with one engine out.

13. What items should the pilot-in-command of a multi-engine aircraft discuss in a typical pre-takeoff briefing when the flight crew consists of two pilots? (FAA-H-8083-3)

The pre-takeoff briefing should consist of at least the following:

a. Minimum control speed (V_{MC});

b. Rotation speed (V_R);

c. Liftoff speed (V_{LOF});

d. Single-engine best rate-of-climb speed (V_{YSE});

e. All-engine best rate-of-climb speed (V_Y);

f. Procedures to be covered if an engine failure occurs below V_{MC}.

14. In the event of an engine failure on takeoff, immediately before liftoff, what procedure is recommended? (FAA-H-8083-3)

If an engine should fail during the takeoff roll before becoming airborne, it is advisable to close both throttles immediately and bring the airplane to a complete stop.

15. If an engine failure occurs immediately after takeoff (gear down) but before reaching the single-engine best rate-of-climb speed (V_{YSE}), what procedure is recommended? (FAA-H-8083-3)

If an engine failure occurs immediately after takeoff, before obtaining single-engine best rate-of-climb speed (V_{YSE}), it is advisable to either land on remaining runway or select a suitable area for landing. An immediate landing is usually inevitable because of the altitude loss required to increase the aircraft speed to V_{YSE}.

16. If an engine failure occurs immediately after takeoff (gear up) but before reaching safe single-engine climb speed, what procedure is recommended? (Assuming no more runway available.) (FAA-H-8083-3)

If the engine-out best angle-of-climb speed (V_{XSE}) has been obtained and the landing gear is in the retract cycle, the pilot should climb at the engine-out best angle-of-climb speed (V_{XSE}) to clear any obstacles, and then stabilize the airspeed at the engine-out best rate-of-climb airspeed (V_{YSE}) while retracting the landing gear and flaps and resetting all appropriate systems.

Note: The above procedures are very generalized—remember that each takeoff is different. Aircraft performance, runway length requirements, etc., should be calculated prior to every takeoff to determine the appropriate course of action for an engine failure at any point during takeoff and climb.

Remember: Most light twins are incapable of sustaining a single-engine climb! Plan accordingly!

17. Following an engine failure on takeoff (airborne) a climb cannot be established. What speed should be used to establish the slowest descent rate? (FAA-H-8083-3)

Single-engine best rate-of-climb speed (V_{YSE}) will provide the maximum altitude gain for a given period of time with one engine operative. Also, if it is apparent a climb cannot be established and an emergency landing is imminent, V_{YSE} will usually produce the slowest rate of descent and provide the most amount of time for executing an emergency landing.

18. In the event of an engine failure immediately after takeoff, which is more important, more altitude or airspeed in excess of V_{YSE} (single-engine best rate-of-climb speed)? (FAA-H-8083-3)

Altitude is more essential to safety after takeoff than is excess airspeed. Excess airspeed cannot be converted readily to the altitude, or the distance necessary to reach a landing area safely in the event of an emergency. In contrast, however, an airplane which has attained a safe altitude will fly in level flight much easier than it will climb. Therefore, if the total energy of both engines is initially used to gain enough height to clear all obstacles while in flight (safe maneuvering altitude), the problem is much simpler in the event an engine fails. If some extra height is available, it usually can be traded for velocity or gliding distance when needed.

19. What is the main problem when an engine fails en route? (FAA-H-8083-3)

When an engine fails en route during cruising flight, the pilot's main problem is to maintain sufficient altitude to be able to continue flight to the point of intended landing. This is dependent upon density altitude, the gross weight of the airplane, and elevation of the terrain and obstructions. When the airplane is above the single-engine service ceiling, altitude will be lost.

20. If an engine failure occurs while en route, what recommended procedure should be followed? (FAA-H-8083-3)

Although engine failure while en route in normal cruise is not considered as critical as in other phases of flight, it is a recommended practice to add maximum permissible power to the operating engine before securing or shutting down the failed engine. If maximum permissible power is not applied, the airspeed may decrease much farther and more rapidly than expected. This condition could present a serious performance problem, especially if the airspeed should drop below V_{YSE} (engine-out best rate-of-climb speed).

The altitude should be maintained if it is within the capability of the airplane. In an airplane not capable of maintaining altitude with an engine inoperative under existing circumstances, the airspeed should be maintained within ± 5 knots of V_{YSE} in order to conserve altitude as long as possible to reach a suitable landing area.

21. In the event of both engines becoming inoperative, what speed should be used to obtain the maximum gliding distance? (Pilot's Operating Handbook)

Maximum gliding distance may be obtained by establishing 110 mph (Cessna 310 at maximum gross weight) and ensuring both propellers are feathered and flaps and gear are up.

22. In the event of an engine failure during the approach and landing phases of flight, what procedures are recommended? (FAA-H-8083-3)

a. The traffic pattern should be identical to a normal traffic pattern.

b. The flight path on base to final should be normal; neither high nor low. Avoid long flat approaches with high power output on the operative engine.

c. Maintain V_{YSE}. Final approach speed should not be less than V_{YSE} until landing is assured; thereafter, it should be at the speed commensurate with the flap position until beginning the roundout or flare.

Continued

   d. Neither full flaps nor landing gear should be extended until
      landing is assured.

   e. With full flaps extended, the approach speed should be 1.3 V_{S0}
      or as recommended by manufacturer.

23. What procedure should be followed in the event of a go-around on one engine?

If the decision is made to execute a go-around, add full power,
retract partial flaps, retract landing gear, retract remaining flaps,
and establish V_{YSE} as soon as possible. When executing a single-
engine go-around, an initial sink rate will occur due to the aircraft
downward momentum and the retraction of flaps and gear, making
it absolutely critical that sufficient altitude be available when the
"Go/No Go" decision is made.

24. Are single-engine go-arounds recommended? Why?
(14 CFR Part 23)

Single-engine go-arounds are generally not recommended. Unless
more than sufficient altitude and airspeed exist, a single-engine
go-around is, for the most part, impossible in light twins certified
under 14 CFR Part 23. Accident statistics indicate a high percent-
age of fatalities occur during single-engine go-arounds as
compared to a controlled crash on or close to the runway, a
taxiway, etc. In most cases, a single-engine go-around is not an
option, considering the particular aircraft, its weight, the density
altitude, etc.

Airplane Systems

3

Some of the following questions are in reference to the systems of a
Cessna 310. For accuracy, you should do a review of your particular
aircraft's Pilot's Operating Handbook.

A. General

1. What is the maximum gross weight of this airplane?

5,535 pounds.

2. What is the maximum takeoff weight of this airplane?

5,500 pounds.

3. What is the maximum landing weight of this airplane?

5,400 pounds.

4. What is the maximum service ceiling of this airplane at gross weight?

19,900 feet.

5. What category was this airplane certificated in?

Normal category.

6. What is the maximum single-engine service ceiling of this airplane?

6,850 feet (single-engine service ceiling increases 425 feet each 30
minutes of flight).

7. Are there any emergency exits and, if so, where are they located?

Yes; the pilot's window on the left side may be jettisoned by
pulling the emergency release ring located under the window and
pushing the window out.

B. Primary Flight Controls and Trim

1. How are the various flight controls operated?

Ailerons—Manually operated through a mechanical linkage consisting of push/pull rods connected from a bell crank to the ailerons and cables connected from the pilot's control yoke to the bell crank.

Elevator—Push/pull rods connect the elevator to a bell crank located in the empennage. Cables connect the pilot's control yoke to the bell crank.

Rudder—A bell crank is attached to the bottom section of the rudder. Cables connect the rudder pedals to the bell crank.

2. What type of trim system is installed in this airplane?

Manually-operated rudder and elevator trim is provided. Both utilize push/pull rods and cables for activation.

3. What procedure should be followed if loss of elevator control occurs?

a. Extend landing gear.

b. Lower 15 degrees of flaps.

c. Trim for level flight.

d. Establish maneuvering speed or approach speed, as appropriate, through use of throttle and elevator trim control.

Do not change the established trim setting. Maintain control of the glide angle by adjusting power. At the landing flare, the elevator trim should be adjusted to full noseup and the power reduced. At the moment of touchdown, close the throttle.

C. Wing Flaps

1. What type of wing flaps are used on this aircraft?

Split flaps.

2. How do the flaps operate?

The flaps are electrically driven and actuated by an electric motor.
They are extended or retracted by positioning the wing flap switch
lever to the desired flap deflection position. A single electric motor
utilizing push/pull rods, two interconnected bell cranks, and cables,
drives both flaps to the selected position. Settings of 0, 15, or 35
degrees may be selected. The wing flap system circuit is protected
by a 15-amp push-to-reset circuit breaker, labeled FLAP.

3. In the event of an emergency, is there a "Manual" flap extension or retraction procedure?

No.

4. What is the maximum degree of flap extension available?

35 degrees.

5. What is the maximum flap extension for takeoff?

15 degrees.

6. What is the maximum flap extension speed?

15 degrees below 180 mph and 15 to 35 degrees below 160 mph.

D. Flight Instruments

1. Which flight instruments are connected to the static system?

The airspeed indicator, altimeter, and vertical speed indicator.

2. Where are the static ports on the airplane?

Two static pressure source holes, one on each side of the rear fuselage, forward of the empennage, provide static pressure for the altimeter, airspeed and vertical speed indicators. Differences in static pressure due to slips, skids, etc. are balanced-out through use of dual static ports.

3. Is there ice protection available for the static system?

No, but a static-pressure alternate-source valve is installed in the static system, providing capability for an alternate static source in the event the external source should become blocked due to ice, etc.

4. What is the source of alternate static air?

Alternate static pressure is supplied from inside the cockpit. When utilizing the alternate static source, the pressure supplied from the cabin will be relatively low, resulting in airspeed and altimeter indications that will be higher than normal.

5. What other function is provided by the static-pressure alternate-source valve?

The valve allows the pilot to drain condensation that may have formed in the static lines.

6. Is there ice protection for the pitot tube?

Yes. The pitot tube, as well as the stall warning transmitter and main fuel tank vents, is equipped with an electrically-heated element. All three are controlled by the pitot heat switch located on the instrument panel.

7. **Which flight instruments are connected to the vacuum system?**

The attitude indicator and directional gyro.

8. **How many vacuum pumps are utilized in the vacuum system?**

One per engine.

9. **Are the vacuum pumps engine-driven or electrically-driven?**

Engine-driven.

10. **What is the required vacuum or pressure required for normal instrument operation?**

4.75 to 5.25 inches of mercury.

11. **How is a vacuum pump failure indicated in this airplane?**

A red indicator on the left or right vacuum gage will extend to indicate failure.

12. **In the event of vacuum pump failure (internal failure, engine failure), is manual selection of the operative vacuum pump required?**

No, a valve will automatically select the operative vacuum source.

13. **During engine-out flight, will the remaining vacuum pump provide enough suction for operation of all systems (instruments, deice, etc.)?**

As always, refer to the aircraft's Pilot's Operating Handbook. In most cases, the remaining vacuum pump will provide sufficient vacuum for normal flight instrument operation; however, other systems such as deice equipment, etc., may have reduced efficiency.

E. Stall Warning System

1. Briefly describe the stall warning system installed on this aircraft.

This aircraft is equipped with a warning transmitter and associated warning horn. The electric transmitter is mounted on the leading edge of the left wing and the horn is mounted behind the instrument panel. The system will energize when the aircraft is within 5 to 10 mph above the stall in all configurations.

Note: The system is inoperative when the battery switch is in the "Off" position. Also, on some aircraft, the stall warning system is deactivated on the ground through use of a relay to the squat switch on the left main landing gear.

2. Does the stall warning system have any protection from icing?

Yes; a heater element is incorporated into the transmitter and is activated anytime the pitot heater switch is in the "On" position.

F. Landing Gear

1. What source of power is utilized by the landing gear system for extension and retraction operations?

An electrically-driven motor.

2. What conditions will cause the gear warning horn to sound?

With the landing gear retracted, the warning horn will sound when:

a. The throttle is retarded to below 12 inches of manifold pressure; and/or

b. The wing flaps are positioned at more than 15 degrees.

3. How is inadvertent gear retraction on the ground prevented?

Accidental gear retraction on the ground is prevented by a safety squat switch located on the left main landing gear shock strut. As long as the strut is compressed, the switch is open, preventing power to the gear motor.

4. How is the gear locked in the "down" position?

The system utilizes mechanical downlocks.

5. How is the gear locked in the "up" position?

The system utilizes mechanical uplocks. Some aircraft may utilize hydraulic pressure.

6. What type of circuit protection is provided for the landing gear system?

A circuit breaker for the landing gear motor is provided.

7. What type of shock absorption is provided for the landing gear?

Hydraulic/pneumatic type struts.

8. The nose wheel can be turned how many degrees to the left or right?

The steerable nose wheel provides positive control up to 15 degrees left or right and free turning from 15 to 55 degrees for sharp turns.

9. How is steering accomplished on the ground?

Steering is accomplished by a steerable nose wheel, interconnected with the rudder system. Differential braking as well as use of differential power may also be used.

10. What are the tire pressures for the main gear and nose wheel tires?

Main tires .... 60 PSI

Nose tire .... 24 PSI

11. Describe the difference between V_{LE} and V_{LO}.

V_{LE}—the maximum calibrated airspeed at which the airplane can be safely flown with the landing gear extended. The landing gear in the extended and locked position can generally withstand higher airloads than when in transit resulting in V_{LE} being higher than V_{LO}.

V_{LO}—the maximum calibrated airspeed at which the landing gear can be safely extended or retracted. V_{LO} is usually lower than V_{LE} because the landing gear components are subjected to higher airloads when extension or retraction is accomplished requiring a reduced airspeed.

12. What particular aircraft component limits the landing gear extension speed?

The nose gear is usually subject to the highest air loads.

13. What are the cockpit indications for landing gear position?

Four gear position indicator lights: 3 green "gear down" indicators (1 for each gear) and 1 red indicator for the "gear unlocked" position.

14. What mechanism is used to cause the gear indicator lights to illuminate when the gear has fully extended and locked?

Electrical contacts are located on each of the main landing gear components. When the gear has extended and locked, the contacts close which causes each respective indicator to illuminate.

15. If one or more landing gear indicator lights have not illuminated and you are reasonably sure the gear has extended and locked, what initial action should be taken?

This situation could be the result of a burned-out bulb. A quick check can be made by using the "press to test" feature incorporated into the light. If the bulb is burned out, or you are still uncertain as to the gear status, a known operative bulb can be used. Also, on some aircraft, when the navigation lights are switched on, the landing gear indicator lights will automatically dim. During the daytime, they may be difficult to see.

16. What is the normal length of time for either landing gear retraction or extension?

5 to 7 seconds.

17. What indications, other than the indicator lights, assist in detection of fully extended landing gear?

a. A change in aircraft pitch will normally occur.

b. The characteristic "bump" will be heard as the gear locks into place.

c. Optional external mirrors for visual confirmation.

18. Why should the brakes be momentarily applied before retraction of the landing gear?

Immediately after takeoff, the rapidly rotating wheels will actually expand in diameter due to centrifugal force. If mud or ice has accumulated in the landing gear wheel wells, the wheels may rub or possibly jam as they enter.

19. Can the landing gear be extended manually? How?

Yes; a hand crank is located below the pilot's seat for manual extension of the gear. To use, extend the crank and lock into position. Check that the landing gear knob (switch) is in the center or neutral position. Pull the landing gear circuit breaker. Rotate the crank clockwise until the gear-down lights are illuminated (approximately 52 turns).

20. Can the landing gear be retracted manually?

No. If attempted, undue loads will be imposed, resulting in excessive wear and possible failure of the cranking mechanism.

21. Is the cabin step retractable or fixed in position?

The cabin step retracts into a well provided for it when the landing gear is retracted. A cable connected to the landing gear actuator enables retraction and a spring provides tension for extension during landing gear extension.

G. Brake System

1. Describe the brake system installed on this aircraft.

The brake system for this aircraft consists of hydraulically actuated disc brakes on both main landing gear. A master cylinder is used for each main wheel, with a hydraulic fluid reservoir for each master cylinder. Braking action is obtained by depressing the top of the rudder pedals. The parking brake uses a valve in each main brake line. When you apply pressure to the top of the rudder pedals while pulling on the parking brake handle, the valve locks pressure on each main brake assembly.

2. On an airplane with hydraulically actuated landing gear, do the brake and landing gear systems share the same hydraulic fluid supply?

Reference the aircraft's POH or AFM.

H. Engine

1. What type of engines power this aircraft?

Continental, 6 cylinder, IO-470 engines.

2. Does this aircraft use fuel injection or carburetion?

Fuel injection.

3. What is the maximum continuous operating power for this type of engine?

260 HP at 2,625 rpm.

4. How is engine cooling accomplished?

External air flow ducted around the engine provides cooling. Some aircraft also utilize cowl flaps to allow for manual control of engine cooling.

5. Where are the intakes for normal induction air located?

Ram air is directed from the front cowling to an air canister filter assembly, and then routed to the fuel air control unit.

6. Does this aircraft have an alternate induction air system? How does it work?

Each engine has an alternate air control available. The controls are located to the right of the control pedestal. When the controls are pushed "in," filtered ram air is provided to the engines. With the controls in the "out" position, unfiltered warm air is provided from inside the engine cowling to the engines.

7. When are the cowl flaps used?

Normally the cowl flaps will be in the OPEN position in the following operations:

a. During starting of the engine.

b. While taxiing.

c. During takeoff and high-power climb operations.

The cowl flaps should be in the CLOSED position in the following operations:

a. During extended letdowns.

b. Anytime excessive cooling is a possibility (i.e., approach to landing, engine-out practice).

The cowl flaps may be adjusted in cruise flight for the appropriate cylinder head temperature.

8. What are normal climb and cruise power settings?

Power and prop settings will vary; refer to the Pilot's Operating Handbook.
Climb at 24 inches MP and 2,450 rpm.
Cruise at 22 inches MP and 2,400 rpm.

9. What is the procedure for starting a flooded engine?

If an engine has been accidentally flooded or overprimed, the following procedure may be used:

Master .... On
Magnetos .... On
Throttle .... Open Full
Mixture .... Idle-cutoff
Starter .... Engage

When the engine fires, move the mixture control to the full rich position and close the throttle to the idle position.

I. Propeller

1. What type of propellers is this airplane equipped with?

The aircraft is equipped with all-metal, constant-speed, full-feathering propellers.

2. What causes the propellers to go to high rpm and low rpm?

Hydraulic pressure and springs/counterweights are utilized to control the pitch of the propellers. Hydraulic pressure from the propeller governor moves the blades to low pitch/high rpm. A set of springs and counterweights move the blades to high pitch/low rpm.

3. What type of hydraulic fluid is used in the propeller system?

Oil from the engine oil system. The oil is boosted by the governor pump and then supplied to the propeller hub.

4. How are the propellers synchronized in flight?

Manually; to synchronize, match the rpm on both engine tachometers. Then adjust the propeller control on one engine until pulsating sound stops.

5. Is there an automatic system for synchronization?

Not usually; however, some aircraft may be equipped with an automatic synchronization system which will usually consist of master and slave engines. The system will automatically compare the speed of the slave engine to the master engine and adjust the speed of the slave until it matches the master engine exactly.

6. What are reversible propellers?

Reversible propellers are used to decrease the total landing roll distance of an aircraft. They are normally found on larger, turbo-prop-type aircraft. The blade angle of a reversible propeller can be changed by the pilot from a "positive" blade angle to a "negative" blade angle which, combined with power from the engine, will create a substantial amount of "reverse" thrust.

7. What does "feathering" a propeller mean?

Feathering a propeller means positioning the blades of the propeller to such a high angle that they are streamlined in the direction of flight. In this feathered position, the blades act as powerful brakes and assist engine friction and compression to stop the windmilling rotation of a propeller.

8. What are the advantages to feathering a propeller?

Feathering a propeller prevents further internal damage as a result of a windmilling propeller. It also reduces the total drag as well as the overall yawing tendency of the airplane, and as a result increases controllability of the airplane.

9. **How long does it normally take for a propeller to feather once the prop control has been placed in the feather position?**

The length of time varies with different makes and models of aircraft. Refer to the Pilot's Operating Handbook for your aircraft. Normally, once the propeller control has been placed in the feather position, the propeller should come to a complete stop within 5 to 10 seconds.

10. **Is this aircraft equipped with an auto-feathering system?**

No. Auto-feathering systems are typically found on turboprop aircraft. They are designed to automatically feather the propeller in the event of a power loss during takeoff and climb phases of flight.

11. **What mechanism causes a propeller to change from a low-pitch condition to a full-feathered position?**

This propeller system utilizes a combination of mechanical springs and counterweights to move the propeller blades to the full-feather position.

12. **What procedure is followed when feathering a propeller on an inoperative engine?**

Inoperative engine side:

Throttle .... Idle
Propeller .... Feather
Mixture .... Idle-cutoff
Fuel selector .... Off
Auxiliary fuel pumps .... Off
Magnetos .... Off
Alternator .... Off

Operative engine side:

Power .... Adjust as necessary
Mixture .... Adjust as necessary
Fuel selector .... Select main tank
Auxiliary fuel pump .... On
Cowl flaps .... As required
Electrical load .... Reduce

13. What are propeller "accumulators"?

Propeller accumulators are used in some multi-engine aircraft to assist in unfeathering the propeller. In the event of an engine failure, no pressure will exist in the governor to assist in unfeathering the propeller. High-pressure oil stored in the accumulator may be used instead of the pressure that would normally be provided by a propeller governor.

14. If accumulators are not used, how is "unfeathering" a propeller accomplished?

Unfeathering a propeller without an accumulator requires the propeller controls to be taken out of the feather position and advanced to the high-rpm position. Following this, the starter should be engaged. This action will result in engine rotation, which will create enough oil pressure to cause the propeller blades to begin to come out of feather. As the blades begin to windmill, the oil pressure will increase, and with ignition, result in a completely unfeathered propeller.

15. How would an in-flight engine restart be accomplished with the propeller in a feathered condition?

Throttle .... Advance until warning horn silent
Propeller .... Set to low pitch/high rpm
Mixture .... Full rich
Magnetos .... On
Starter .... Engage, if necessary

16. Why won't a propeller go into feathered position when the engine is shut down on the ground?

Because of a spring-loaded centrifugal latch mechanism — when engine speed falls below a certain rpm (600 to 800 rpm), the latch mechanism is no longer held open by centrifugal force (as with a windmilling propeller in the air or idling engine on the ground). A spring causes the latch to engage, preventing the propeller from going to a feathered position.

17. **Is it possible for the centrifugal latch mechanism to prevent feathering a propeller after an engine failure in flight?**

    After an engine failure in flight, the windmilling propeller creates enough centrifugal force to prevent the latch mechanism from engaging until the pilot decides to feather the propeller.

J. Fuel System

1. **Where are the fuel tanks located?**

   The main tanks are located on the wing tips. Optional auxiliary tanks are located in each wing outboard of each engine nacelle.

2. **What are the capacities of the fuel tanks, both usable and total?**

   Main Tanks .... 102 gallons total, 100 gallons usable
   Auxiliary Tanks .... 41 gallons total, 40 gallons usable

3. **How many fuel pumps are utilized in the aircraft fuel system?**

   6 pumps: 1 engine-driven fuel pump per engine; 1 main tank auxiliary pump per engine; 1 fuel transfer pump in each main tank.

4. **Are the fuel pumps engine-driven or electrical?**

   2 engine-driven pumps and 4 electrically-driven pumps.

5. **When are the electric auxiliary fuel pumps used?**

   They are used for engine priming during the start procedure and provide fuel to the engine should an engine-driven pump fail.

6. Where are the fuel selector valves located?

The fuel selector valves are located on the floor between the pilot and copilot seats. Placards indicate LEFT ENGINE OFF, LEFT MAIN, and RIGHT MAIN for the left engine fuel selector and RIGHT ENGINE OFF, RIGHT MAIN, and LEFT MAIN for the right engine fuel selector.

7. Where are the fuel vents located?

The fuel vents are located on the bottom of each tip tank.

8. Where are the fuel sumps (drains) located?

Three drains per side are provided:

a. Fuel tank drains (located on tip tanks)

b. Auxiliary fuel tank drains (under the wing under the auxiliary tanks)

c. Fuel line crossover drains (under the wing near the wing root)

9. If a vapor return system is incorporated into the fuel system, what tank will receive the recovered fuel?

Any vapor or excess fuel will be returned to the main tanks.

10. How is the fuel quantity measured and indicated?

This system consists of one fuel quantity indicator per tank, and one fuel sensor unit per tank. The electrical fuel indicators measure fuel in gallons and pounds. Also, a switch allows selection of which tank's (main or auxiliary) fuel quantity will be indicated.

11. What are the minimum and maximum fuel pressures and fuel flows?

2.5 to 20.10 PSI and 0 to 23 GPH.

12. Describe auxiliary fuel pump operation.

Electrically-actuated auxiliary pumps are provided. The pumps provide fuel under pressure for priming during engine starts, as well as fuel to the engine in the event of an engine-driven pump failure. In most Cessna aircraft, the auxiliary fuel pumps may be selected to operate in LOW, ON, or OFF mode. In the LOW position, the pump operates at low pressure regardless of the situation. When selected to the ON position, the pumps operate in the low pressure mode but, in the event of an engine-driven pump failure, will automatically switch to high pressure to provide adequate fuel flow for engine operation.

Note: Some Cessna multi-engine aircraft are equipped with auxiliary fuel pumps that have a two-position rocker switch. The pumps may be selected to either an ON or OFF position. In the ON position the pump will provide either low or high pressure depending on the current condition. Low pressure is provided when the switch is in the ON position. High pressure is provided when fuel pressure drops below 5 PSI, the throttle is set to at least 15 to 18 inches manifold pressure and the auxiliary pump switch is ON.

13. When is use of the auxiliary fuel pumps recommended?

The situations dictating use of the auxiliary fuel pumps vary from aircraft to aircraft. The Pilot's Operating Handbook should always be referred to for the correct procedure. Generally, the use of the auxiliary fuel pumps is recommended in the following conditions:

a. During ground operations on hot days, when vapor lock problems may exist;

b. On every takeoff and initial climb;

c. When switching fuel tanks;

d. When fuel pressure fluctuation occurs followed by rough engine operation;

e. High-altitude operations (refer to POH);

f. When an engine-driven pump fails;

g. During approach and landing operations.

14. Where are the auxiliary fuel pumps located?

The electric auxiliary pumps are submerged in the main fuel tanks.

15. What engine performance may be expected when using the auxiliary fuel pumps?

When the auxiliary fuel pumps are operating in the HI mode, the fuel/air mixture will be excessively rich and, as a result, less than best power will be obtained. Typically the mixture must be adjusted to obtain smooth engine operation.

16. What are the fuel transfer pumps used for?

These pumps are installed in each main tip tank. Their function is to provide a continuous fuel supply from the tip tanks to the engines during high angles of descent.

17. During preflight inspection, how can the fuel transfer pumps be checked for normal operation?

With the battery switch on, the pumps can be heard by listening for a pulsing sound emanating from the main tip tanks.

18. What is recommended procedure for fuel management during extended flights?

During the enroute phase of flight, it is desirable to burn fuel evenly on both sides so that a balanced fuel load is available for approach and landing. Pilots should be alert for unequal fuel flow situations as a result of uncoordinated flight, single-engine flight, etc., and if necessary, should balance the fuel load by operating both engines from the heavier tank until balance is achieved. It is possible that during approach and landing maneuvers, if fuel has not been managed properly, the fuel remaining may not be sufficient to provide a continuous supply of fuel to the fuel supply outlet. A loss of power may result.

19. What procedure is recommended concerning use of fuel in the auxiliary tanks during extended flights?

It is generally recommended that fuel be fed to the engines from both the auxiliary and main tank evenly rather than running a fuel tank dry. Sediment, water, etc., in the bottom of the tank may cause rough engine operation or engine stoppage when running a fuel tank dry.

20. Why is it recommended procedure to switch fuel tanks prior to the before-takeoff engine runup?

The practice of switching tanks immediately before takeoff may not provide enough time to guarantee that uninterrupted fuel flow will be provided on the newly selected tanks. The engines could possibly continue to function normally on the fuel remaining in the lines before failing on the takeoff roll or climb. To ensure that the engines will operate on the selected tanks for departure, changing tanks should be accomplished well before the before-takeoff checklist (during taxi).

21. Is it possible to crossfeed fuel from one engine to the other?

Yes; fuel may be obtained from either main tank and directed to the left or right engine. Fuel from the left or right auxiliary tanks can only be used by the respective engine on the same side as the auxiliary tank. Crossfeed operations are possible by positioning the fuel selector valve on the inoperative engine (for example, right side) to OFF and positioning the fuel selector valve on the operative engine (left side) to right.

22. What type of problems will result if crossfeed operations are not utilized after an engine failure en route?

a. Obviously, aircraft range would be limited on one fuel tank.

b. Trim problems due to one wing being heavier (more fuel) than the other.

23. In the event of an engine-driven fuel pump failure, what procedure should be followed?

Auxiliary fuel pump .... ON
Mixture .... Adjust for optimum engine performance

24. Be able to draw a detailed diagram of the aircraft fuel system.

K. Hydraulic System

1. What equipment would be considered hydraulic on this aircraft?

a. A hydraulically-actuated brake on each main gear

b. An air/oil nose gear shock strut

c. Constant-speed propellers

Some aircraft may also use hydraulic systems for extension and retraction of the landing gear and/or flaps. Refer to the Pilot's Operating Handbook for your particular aircraft.

2. What provides hydraulic power to the landing gear system?

A typical hydraulic extension system uses either an electrically-driven hydraulic power-pack or an engine-driven hydraulic pump.

3. Describe the components of any hydraulic landing system.

Hydraulic systems usually consist of the following:

a. A hydraulic power-pack, either electrically- or engine-driven.

b. A hydraulic reservoir containing fluid for system operation.

c. Hydraulic actuators or cylinders which use hydraulic pressure.

d. Switches which regulate or direct hydraulic pressure in the system.

L. Electrical System

1. What is the electrical system voltage?

This aircraft has a 28-volt, negative-ground, DC system.

2. What voltage is required for starting from the battery?

24 volts.

3. Where is the battery located?

The battery is located in the left wing, outboard of the engine nacelle.

4. Why is starting the left engine first standard operating procedure on most multi-engine aircraft?

The cable from the battery to the engine is shorter on the left side than on the right side. This allows for more electrical current to be supplied to the starter.

5. Does this aircraft utilize generators or alternators?

Alternators.

6. What is the rated amperage of the alternators or generators?

The alternators utilized for this aircraft are rated at 50 amps.

7. Does this aircraft have an APU receptacle and if so, where is it located?

Yes. External DC power may be connected to a receptacle located on the lower surface of the left nacelle baggage compartment.

8. What is the start procedure when using external power for starting?

a. Alternator and battery switches off.

b. Connect the external power source.

c. Switch magnetos on.

d. Start left engine.

e. Disconnect external power source.

f. Alternator and battery switches on.

g. Start right engine.

9. During the before-takeoff static runup what is the normal drop expected when checking the magnetos?

Always refer to the Pilot's Operating Handbook for your aircraft. Normally the pilot should expect between 100 and 175 rpm drop with a difference of no more than 50 rpm, when comparing one magneto with the other.

10. How is the output of each of the alternators equalized?

Voltage regulators control the voltage output of each alternator.

11. What distributes electrical power throughout the airplane?

Buss bars.

12. How is a high/low voltage condition indicated in the cockpit?

A voltammeter and indicators are provided on the instrument panel.

13. How is an alternator failure detected?

One alternator failure sensor is provided per alternator. In the event of an alternator failure, or an overvoltage/undervoltage condition, the sensor will detect and illuminate the appropriate indicator on the instrument panel.

14. If one alternator becomes inoperative, what procedure should you follow?

a. Check and reset the alternator circuit breaker.

b. If the circuit breaker is re-opened, ensure that it remains open and switch off the inoperative alternator.

c. If the circuit breaker does not re-open, monitor the alternator output on the voltammeter. If the output fluctuates or appears abnormally low or high, turn off the alternator.

d. Reduce electrical load.

e. Land as soon as possible.

15. If excessive voltage occurs in the system, what safety feature in the electrical system takes the alternator off-line?

An overvoltage relay is provided. In the event an excessive voltage (32 volts) occurs in the system, the overvoltage relay will be tripped disabling the alternator. The relay may be reset by recycling the alternator switch from ON to OFF to ON.

16. What is the function of the Emergency Power Switch?

In the event both alternators become inoperative due to a battery relay failure, an emergency power switch is provided which will supply enough power from the battery to re-excite the alternators.

M. Environmental System

1. What type of cabin heating system is this aircraft equipped with?

The cabin heating system consists of the following:

a. An air inlet

b. A combustion-type heater

c. A ventilating fan

d. Controllable outlets located in the cabin

2. How does the cabin heating system operate?

Outside air is ducted from the front opening on the right side of the nose to a combustion-type heater where it is heated and then ducted to the pilot/passenger compartments. It is exhausted overboard through an outlet in the passenger compartment.

3. How is cabin temperature controlled?

The cabin air temperature control knob adjusts a thermostat that controls the temperature in a duct located aft of the heater. When the temperature of the air exceeds the thermostat setting, the thermostat shuts down the heater. When the air temperature equals the thermostat setting the heater is reactivated.

4. If a combustion-type heater is utilized, fuel is provided from what source, and how much fuel is used per hour?

The cabin heater receives fuel from a tee in the fuel crossfeed line. Fuel pressure is supplied by a fuel pump mounted on the heater assembly. Fuel consumption is approximately 0.3 gallons per hour.

5. What are the indications of a heater overheating?

An amber overheat warning light is provided.

6. By what method is a combustion-type heater prevented from a potentially dangerous overheated condition?

A heater overheat switch is provided. When the air in the heater has exceeded 325°F, the overheat switch is actuated and the indicator light is illuminated. The switch automatically turns the heater off, and the heater cannot be reactivated without first resetting the switch (located in the right forward nose compartment).

7. Where is the external inlet located for cabin air?

On the right side of the nose.

8. Where are the cabin heat/air vents located within the cabin?

2 outlets at the base of the windshield;

1 outlet in the forward cabin bulkhead;

1 on each side of the forward cabin;

2 outlets located in the aft passenger compartment on the aft face of the main spar.

9. By what method is fuel prevented from flowing to a combustion-type heater that is not in operation?

The cabin heater receives its fuel from the aircraft fuel system via a fuel pump mounted on the heater assembly. As long as the cabin heat switch is in the OFF position, fuel will not be supplied to the cabin heater.

N. Oil System

1. Briefly describe the engine oil system.

The oil system for this aircraft is a wet-sump pressure-type system.

2. What are the minimum and maximum safe oil capacities?

The minimum oil level is 9 quarts for local flight operations and 12 quarts for flights of more than 2 hours. The maximum capacity of the oil sump is 13 quarts (includes 1 quart in the oil filter).

3. What are the minimum and maximum oil temperatures and pressures?

Oil Temperature Gage

Normal Operating Range .... 75° to 240°F
Maximum Temperature .... 240°F

Oil Pressure Gage

Idling Pressure .... 10 PSI
Normal Operating Range .... 30 to 60 PSI
Maximum Pressure .... 100 PSI

4. Are the oil temperature and pressure gages electric or mechanical?

The oil temperature gages are electric, and the oil pressure gages are direct-reading mechanical gages.

5. What type of oil is used in this system?

Above 40°F .... SAE 50
Below 40°F .... SAE 10W30 or SAE 30

O. Deice and Anti-Ice System

1. What type of deice or anti-ice system is provided for the propellers?

None; some light aircraft will utilize anti-icing fluid for the propeller. The centrifugal force produced by the propeller as well as the anti-icing agents in the fluid are extremely effective in removing and preventing further ice development. Also, some aircraft may use electrically-heated boots for ice propeller removal and prevention.

2. If the aircraft is not equipped with propeller deice, what procedures should be followed to prevent propeller ice from forming?

These actions may be taken to help prevent and reduce ice formation:

a. Increase engine speed; higher rpm increases centrifugal force.

b. Cycle the propeller rpm to flex the propeller blades.

3. What type of deice or anti-ice is provided for the leading edges of the aircraft?

If equipped, a pneumatic system is typically used on light aircraft. It may consist of engine-driven vacuum pumps, electrical timers, pressure switches and inflatable rubber deice boots.

4. What is the source of power for the deice or anti-ice system?

Deice and anti-ice systems might use the following:

Pneumatic—Pressurized air from the pressure side of a vacuum pump inflates mechanical boots on the leading edges of the wing and tail surfaces.

Hot Air—Obtained from the compressor section of a turbojet or turboprop engine.

Electrical—Electrically-heated elements embedded in rubber, Plexiglas, etc., may be attached to propellers, windshields, etc.

5. Is there a deice or anti-ice system for the windshield?

No. If equipped, this system typically consists of an electrically operated pump with tubes located near the windshield which disperse the anti-ice fluid (alcohol) contained in an internal reservoir. The system is actuated by an electrical switch in the cockpit. Another system uses electrically-heated wires embedded in the windshield or Plexiglas attached to the windshield.

6. Is there protection from induction-air icing?

No, but an alternate induction system is provided and should be utilized anytime temperatures fall below 35°F with visible moisture present, or when the temperature is below 35°F and the temperature/dewpoint spread is less than 5°. Use of alternate intake air will result in a decrease in engine power due to higher induction air temperatures, so this should be done only when icing conditions are suspected.

P. Autopilot System

1. What type of autopilot system is installed?

A two-axis autopilot system capable of controlling both bank and pitch.

2. What are the basic features of the autopilot?

a. Automatic tracking of a selected magnetic heading.

b. Automatic tracking of a selected VOR radial or ILS localizer/ glide slope.

c. Altitude hold; automatic pitch and trim control enabling altitude selected to be maintained.

3. What aircraft system failures will cause the autopilot to operate erratically?

a. Roll and yaw motions are sensed by the turn coordinator. Failure of this instrument's gyro due to internal failure will result in problems with the autopilot system.

b. Vacuum system failure will cause problems with heading control since the directional gyro is used for heading information.

c. Static system blockage will result in erroneous information received by the altitude sensor, causing problems when operating in the "altitude hold" mode.

4. In the event of an autopilot malfunction, what emergency procedure is used to disable it?

In an emergency, simply select OFF on the autopilot on-off switch. If this does not disengage the autopilot system, pull the associated circuit breaker for that system. As a very last resort, the Master Switch may be temporarily switched to OFF.

5. Is it possible to manually overpower the autopilot?

Yes; the autopilot system may be physically overpowered at any time without damage to the servos.

6. Can the autopilot be used in the event of a single-engine emergency?

No.

Multi-Engine Maneuvers

4

The following information was derived from the Practical Test Standards FAA-S-8081-14M. For accuracy, a review of the PTS applicable to your particular certification check should be made (i.e., Commercial, Instrument).

A. Before-Takeoff Check

1. Position airplane properly considering other aircraft, wind, and surface conditions.

2. Divide attention inside and outside cockpit.

3. Ensure engine temperatures and pressures are suitable for runup and takeoff.

4. Accomplish before-takeoff checklist and confirm airplane is in a safe operating condition.

5. Review takeoff performance airspeeds, takeoff distances, emergency procedures and departure procedure.

6. Ensure no conflict with traffic prior to taxiing into takeoff position.

7. Complete the appropriate checklist.

B. Normal and Crosswind Takeoff and Climb

1. Position flight controls for existing wind conditions and set flaps as recommended.

2. Clear the area and taxi into takeoff position aligning airplane on runway centerline.

3. Advance throttle smoothly to takeoff power; check engine instruments.

4. Rotate at recommended airspeed and liftoff.

5. Accelerate to and establish the pitch attitude for V_Y and maintain V_Y, +10, -5 knots.

6. Retract landing gear and flaps after a positive rate of climb is established.

7. Maintain takeoff power and best rate-of-climb airspeed to safe maneuvering altitude.

Continued

8. Set climb power and transition to recommended climb airspeed.

9. Maintain directional control and proper wind drift correction.

10. Comply with noise abatement procedures.

11. Complete the appropriate checklist.

C. Normal and Crosswind Approach and Landing

1. Approaching traffic pattern, perform "in range" checklist.

2. Establish recommended approach and landing configuration and airspeed.

3. Enter traffic pattern at appropriate airspeed and altitude.

4. On downwind, maintain traffic pattern airspeed and set flaps for approach.

5. Opposite touchdown, gear down and complete before-landing checklist.

6. On final, set flaps for landing, and complete before-landing checklist again.

7. Maintain a stabilized approach and recommended airspeed or, in its absence, not more than 1.3 V_{S0}, +10, -5 knots with gust factor applied.

8. Touchdown smoothly at approximate stalling speed, at or within 400 feet beyond a specified point.

9. Touchdown with no drift and with the airplane longitudinal axis aligned with and over runway centerline.

10. Maintain crosswind correction and directional control throughout approach and landing.

11. Complete appropriate checklist.

D. Short-Field Takeoff and Climb

1. Position flight controls for existing wind conditions and set flaps as recommended.

2. Clear the area and taxi into takeoff position, aligning airplane on runway centerline.

3. Position aircraft to allow use of all available runway.

4. Advance throttle smoothly to takeoff power; check engine instruments.

5. Rotate at recommended airspeed and liftoff.

6. Accelerate to and establish the pitch attitude for the recommended obstacle clearance airspeed or V_X.

7. Maintain recommended obstacle clearance airspeed, or V_X, +10, -5 knots until obstacle cleared or until airplane is 50 feet (20 meters) above the surface.

8. After clearing obstacle accelerate to V_Y, maintain V_Y, +10, -5 knots during climb.

9. Retract landing gear and flaps after a positive rate of climb is established.

10. Maintain takeoff power and best rate-of-climb airspeed to safe maneuvering altitude.

11. Set climb power and transition to recommended climb airspeed.

12. Maintain directional control and proper wind drift correction.

13. Comply with any noise abatement procedure.

14. Complete appropriate checklist.

E. Short-Field Approach and Landing

1. Approaching traffic pattern, perform "in range" checklist.

2. Establish recommended approach and landing configuration and airspeed.

3. Enter traffic pattern at appropriate airspeed and altitude.

4. On downwind, maintain traffic pattern airspeed and set flaps for approach.

5. Opposite touchdown, gear down and complete before-landing checklist.

6. On final, set flaps for landing, and complete before-landing checklist again.

7. Maintain a stabilized approach and recommended airspeed or, in its absence, not more than 1.3 V_{S0}, +10, -5 knots with gust factor applied.

8. Touch down smoothly at approximate stalling speed, at or within 200 feet beyond a specified point.

9. Touchdown with no drift and with the airplane's longitudinal axis aligned with and over runway centerline.

10. Apply brakes as necessary, to stop in the shortest distance consistent with safety.

11. Maintain crosswind correction and directional control throughout approach and landing.

12. Complete appropriate checklist.

F. Go-Around

1. Apply takeoff power immediately.

2. Establish pitch attitude for V_Y, +10, -5 knots.

3. Retract flaps to approach setting.

4. Retract landing gear after a positive rate of climb is established.

5. Maintain takeoff power and V_Y to a safe maneuvering altitude.

6. Set power and transition to airspeed appropriate for traffic pattern.

7. Maintain directional control and wind drift correction throughout climb.

8. Comply with any noise abatement procedures.

9. Maneuver aircraft to comply with appropriate traffic pattern.

10. Complete appropriate checklists as required.

G. Steep Turns

1. Select an altitude no lower than 3,000 feet (920 meters) AGL.

2. Establish the manufacturer's recommended airspeed or if one is not stated, the examiner may designate a safe airspeed not to exceed V_A.

3. Clear the area for other air traffic.

4. Establish a specific heading (cardinal heading N,S,E,W).

5. Roll into a coordinated 360-degree turn.

6. Maintain 45 degrees of bank, ±5 degrees.

7. Roll out on the entry heading, ±10 degrees.

8. Roll into a 360-degree turn in the opposite direction.

9. Divide attention between airplane control and orientation.

10. Maintain the entry altitude, ±100 feet (30 meters), and airspeed, ±10 knots.

H. Maneuvering During Slow Flight

1. Select an altitude no lower than 3,000 feet (920 meters) AGL or recommended altitude, whichever is higher.

2. Clear the area for other air traffic.

3. Establish appropriate power setting and pitch attitude for slow flight.

4. Stabilize airspeed at 10 knots, +10, -5 knots, above 1.2 V_{S1} or V_{MC}, whichever is greater.

5. Establish coordinated straight-and-level flight and level turns, at various bank angles and configurations.

6. Establish coordinated climbs and descents, straight and turning, at various bank angles and configurations.

7. Divide attention between airplane control and orientation.

8. Maintain specified altitude, ±100 feet (30 meters); the specified heading, ±10 degrees; and the specified airspeed, +10, -5 knots.

9. Maintain specified angle of bank, not to exceed 30 degrees in level flight, +0, -10 degrees; maintain the specified angle of bank, not to exceed 20 degrees in climbing or descending flight, +0, -10 degrees; roll out on specified heading, ±10 degrees; level off from climbs and descents within ±100 feet (30 meters).

I. Power-Off Stalls

1. Select an altitude no lower than 3,000 feet (920 meters) AGL or recommended altitude, whichever is higher.

2. Clear the area for other air traffic.

3. Establish a stabilized approach in the approach and landing configuration.

4. Transition smoothly from approach and landing attitude to pitch attitude that will induce a stall.

5. Maintain specific heading, ±10 degrees, if in straight and level flight; maintain a specific bank angle not to exceed 30 degrees, +0, -10 degrees, if in turning flight while inducing stall.

6. Recognize and announce the first aerodynamic indications of an oncoming stall; i.e., buffeting or decay of control effectiveness.

7. Recover promptly after a stall occurs by simultaneously decreasing the pitch attitude, applying power, and leveling the wings to return to a straight-and-level flight attitude with a minimum loss of altitude.

8. Retract flaps to recommended setting.

9. Retract landing gear after a positive rate of climb is established.

10. Accelerate to V_Y, before final flap retraction.

11. Return to entry altitude, heading, and airspeed.

J. Power-On Stalls

1. Select an altitude no lower than 3,000 feet (920 meters) AGL or recommended altitude, whichever is higher.

2. Clear the area for other air traffic.

3. Establish a takeoff or departure configuration, airspeed, and power.

4. Transition smoothly from takeoff or departure attitude to pitch attitude that will induce a stall.

5. Maintain specific heading, ±10 degrees, if in straight and level flight; maintain a specific bank angle not to exceed 20 degrees, +0, -10 degrees, if in turning flight while inducing stall.

6. Recognize and announce the first aerodynamic indications of an oncoming stall; i.e., buffeting or decay of control effectiveness.

7. Recover promptly after a stall occurs by simultaneously decreasing the pitch attitude, applying power as appropriate, and leveling the wings to return to a straight-and-level flight attitude with a minimum loss of altitude.

8. Retract flaps to recommended setting.

9. Retract landing gear after a positive rate of climb is established.

10. Accelerate to V_Y, before final flap retraction.

11. Return to entry altitude, heading, and airspeed.

K. Emergency Descent

1. Establish recommended emergency descent configuration and airspeed.

2. Maintain airspeed, ±5 knots.

3. Maintain orientation, division of attention and proper planning.

4. Follow appropriate emergency checklist.

L. Maneuvering With One Engine Inoperative

1. Recognize engine failure, maintain control and follow recommended emergency procedure.

2. Set engine controls, reduce drag, and identify and verify inoperative engine.

3. Establish recommended best engine inoperative airspeed.

4. Bank toward operating engine as required for best performance, trim airplane and maintain control.

5. Attempt to determine reason for engine malfunction.

6. Feather propeller of inoperative engine.

7. Monitor operating engine and make adjustments as necessary.

8. Follow appropriate checklist to verify procedures for securing inoperative engine.

9. Turn toward the nearest suitable airport.

10. With one engine inoperative (propeller feathered) demonstrate:
    a. straight-and-level flight
    b. turns in both directions
    c. descents to assigned altitudes
    d. climbs to assigned altitudes (if airplane is capable of climbing under existing conditions)

11. Divide attention between coordinated control, the flightpath and orientation.

12. Perform an engine restart in accordance with recommended procedures.

13. Maintain the specific altitude, ±100 feet (30 meters); the specific heading, ±10 degrees; and the specified airspeed, ±10 knots.

14. Maintain specific bank angle, ±10 degrees; roll out on specific heading, ±10 degrees; and levels off from climbs and descents within ±100 feet (30 meters).

Note: The feathering of one propeller shall be demonstrated in multi-engine airplanes equipped with propellers which can be safely feathered in flight. An appropriately-equipped airplane shall be provided by the applicant. This shall be performed at altitudes, in areas and from positions where safe landings on established airports can be readily accomplished, in the event difficulty is encountered in unfeathering and/or restarting. A propeller that cannot be unfeathered during the practical test shall be treated as an emergency. At altitudes lower than 3,000 feet (920 meters) AGL, simulated engine failure shall be performed by throttling the engine back to idle and then establishing zero thrust.

M. Engine Inoperative—Loss of Directional Control Demonstration

1. Configure the airplane at V_{SSE} as follows:
   a. Landing gear retracted
   b. Flaps set for takeoff
   c. Cowl flaps set for takeoff
   d. Trim set for takeoff
   e. Propellers set for high rpm
   f. Power on critical engine reduced to idle
   g. Power on the operating engine set to takeoff or maximum available power.

2. Establish single engine climb attitude with airspeed at approximately 10 knots above V_{SSE}.

3. Establish a bank toward the operating engine, required for best performance.

Continued

4. Increase the pitch attitude slowly to reduce the airspeed, at approximately 1 knot per second, while applying rudder to maintain directional control until full rudder is applied.

5. Recognize and announce the first indications of loss of directional control, stall warning or buffet.

6. Recover promptly by simultaneously reducing power sufficiently on the operating engine while decreasing the angle of attack as necessary to regain airspeed and directional control with a minimum loss of altitude. Recovery *should not* be attempted by increasing the power on the simulated failed engine.

7. Recover within 20 degrees of entry heading.

8. Accelerate to V_{XSE}/V_{YSE}, as appropriate, +10, -5 knots during recovery.

N. Engine Failure During Takeoff Before V_{MC} (Simulated)

1. Close throttles smoothly and promptly after simulated failure.

2. Maintain directional control.

3. Apply braking as necessary.

O. Engine Failure After Lift-Off (Simulated)

1. Recognize engine failure promptly, maintain control and follow recommended emergency procedure.

2. Reduce drag, identify and verify inoperative engine after simulated failure.

3. Simulate feathering the propeller of inoperative engine.

4. Establish V_{YSE}; if obstructions are present, establish V_{XSE} or V_{MC}, +10 knots, whichever is greater, until obstructions are cleared, then transition to V_{YSE}.

5. Bank toward the operative engine as required for best performance, trim airplane and maintain control.

6. Monitor operating engine and make adjustments as necessary.

7. Recognize airplane's performance capabilities. If a climb is not possible at V_{YSE}, maintain V_{YSE} and return to the departure airport for a landing or initiate an approach to the most suitable landing area available.

8. Secure inoperative engine if appropriate.

9. Maintain heading, ±10 degrees, and airspeed, +10, -5 knots.

10. Complete appropriate emergency checklist.

P. Approach and Landing With an Inoperative Engine (Simulated)

1. Recognize engine failure, maintain control, and follow recommended emergency procedure.

2. Set engine controls, reduce drag, and identify and verify inoperative engine after simulated engine failure.

3. Simulate feathering the propeller of inoperative engine.

4. Establish the recommended best engine inoperative airspeed, +10, -5 knots.

5. Bank toward operative engine as required for best performance, trim the airplane and maintain control.

6. Monitor the operating engine and make adjustments as necessary.

7. Establish recommended best engine inoperative approach landing configuration, and airspeed.

8. Maintain a stabilized approach and recommended approach airspeed, +10, -5 knots of V_{YSE} until landing is ensured.

9. Touchdown smoothly at or within 500 feet beyond a specified point, with no drift, and with the airplane's longitudinal axis aligned with and over the runway centerline.

10. Maintain crosswind correction and directional control throughout the approach and landing.

11. Complete the appropriate emergency checklist.

Notes

Notes

More Pilot Products from ASA

ASA has many other books and supplies for pilots; they're listed below, and are available from an aviation retailer in your area. Need help locating a retailer? Call ASA at **1-800-ASA-2-FLY**. We can also send you our latest ASA Catalog, which includes our complete line of publications and pilot supplies... for all types of pilots and aviation technicians.

Also available:
The Complete Advanced Pilot
(for Commercial and Instrument)
#ASA-CAP-2 .... $24.95

The Complete Multi-Engine Pilot
by Bob Gardner

This new edition provides a complete multi-engine flight training program, including new review questions for each chapter. Applicable to both U.S. and European multi-engine training programs, the book has three new appendices: a multi-engine rating syllabus for an integrated flight/ground training program, a new written exam for use when checking out in a new twin, and reprints of applicable FAA advisory circulars and source material for further study on all aspects of multi-engine training. Foreword by Barry Schiff. Index, glossary, 182 pages. ISBN 1-56027-334-8
#ASA-MPT-2 .... $19.95

2000 FAR/AIM Series

For more than a decade, ASA's FAR/AIM Series has been the respected source of government regulations organized specifically for pilots and technicians.

Important features of ASA's FAR/AIM Series:

- Page numbering system for quick and easy reference
- Easy-to-read fonts, yet still convenient book size
- All Parts cite the dates written and amended
- All changes since last printing clearly identified in contents and within text
- Contents organized and consistent throughout text
- Free Midyear Updates available through mail-in coupon or by phone
- Provides the most pertinent Parts at the most reasonable price for maximum value
- All three books available in boxes of 12 for retailers.

FAR/AIM .... #ASA-00-FR-AM-BK $15.95
FAR for Flight Crew .... #ASA-00-FAR-FC $16.95
FAR for Aviation Maintenance Technicians ..... #ASA-00-FAR-AMT $18.95

Prices subject to change without notice.

For a free catalog of ASA's complete product line, call **1-800-ASA-2-FLY**.